Up to Speed

Also by Rae Armantrout

POETRY:

Veil: New and Selected Poems

The Pretext

Made to Seem

Necromance

Couverture

Precedence

The Invention of Hunger

Extremities

MEMOIR:

True

Up to Speed

Rae Armantrout

Wesleyan Univeristy Press

MIDDLETOWN, CONNECTICUT

Published by Wesleyan University Press, Middletown, CT 06459
Printed in the United States of America
5 4 3 2 1

ACKNOWLEDGMENTS
These poems have appeared in the following magazines and anthologies: *American Women Poets in the 21st Century, Best American Poetry of 2002, Chain, Chicago Review, Conduit, Conjunctions, Electronic Poetry Review, Facture, Fence, Germ, Jacket, Kiosk, Mississippi Review, No Journal, Place as Purpose, Ribot, Sal Mimeo, Shiny, The Boston Review, The Gig, The Great American Prose Poem: Poe to the Present, Washington Square,* and *XCP: Cross-Cultural Poetics.* The author would like to thank the editors of these anthologies and journals and the California Arts Council for support.

Library of Congress Cataloging-in-Publication Data

Armantrout, Rae, 1947–
  Up to speed / by Rae Armantrout.
    p. cm. — (Wesleyan poetry)
  ISBN 0–8195–6697–7 (cloth : alk. paper) — ISBN 0–8195–6698–5 (pbk. : alk. paper)
  I. Title. II. Series.
  PS3551.R455U6 2004
  811'.54—dc22   2003017527

CONTENTS

Up to Speed

UP TO SPEED

Streamline to instantaneous
voucher in/voucher out
system.

The plot winnows.

The Sphinx
wants me to guess.

Does a road
run its whole length
at once?

Does a creature
curve to meet
itself?

Whirlette!

*

Covered or cupboard
breast? Real

housekeeping's
kinesthesiac. Cans

held high
to counterbalance "won't."

Is it
such agendas

which survive
as souls?

*

Vagueness is personal!

A wall of concrete bricks,
right here,
while sun surveys its grooves

and I try
"instantly" then "forever."

But the word is
way back,
show-boating.

Light is "with God"

(light, the traveler).

*

Are you the come-on
and the egress?

One who hobbles by
determinedly?

Not yet?

FORM

Dear April, I appreciated the way the paragraphs were all about the same
length. I especially liked how your sentences appeared
to relate to one another. It was getting late,
they said. Solemn,
blunt flash of sun
off the window
of a Coors Light
truck.

On a fence across the street, wings of a wooden chicken
spun backward. Everyone
had reason to be proud.
I could handle symbols
without being manipulated by them.
Like a stone butch, you might say, but that's
only connotation.

Meanwhile, in the photographs,
my expression was fading,
as if my darling,
Ambiguity,
were just another word
for death

What is the nature of the resting state
but gaseous longing/
regret?
In the original/
final form—

without objects

CURRENCY

I stare at the edge

until the word
tulip

comes up
where I thought it might.

But the lag-time
is a problem.

The swollen, yellow
head of Tweety-Bird

now offered
at the border

as balloon
or ceramic,

as baby
plus crucifixion,

as distended
incredulity

held toward the cars,
as silence

EXCEPTIONAL

The one who hasn't grabbed a seat
when the music stops

will be known as
"matter" or "universe."

     *

An incredible sequence
of articulated sores

erupts

from the bony
brown arm
of the rose

(except that there *are* no
sequences.)

     *

Sweet, rounded
shoulders of the road,

shiny with pieces
of metal and glass,

take an eternity,

a projected
future-perfect retrospect,

except

SAKE

In order to be found—
or *recognized*—

one must repeat
a passage at some length.

*

"Why do Princesses
Caroline and Stephanie

always marry
the wrong men?"

*

Repeated passages
are gathered

as if
for their own sakes.

*

A child's cry breaks
into spires
and alcoves;

glass
is stained.

*

From here on
it's *all* metaphor

(self
as repertoire)

*

Music extends "at once"

how far?

AFTERLIFE

1

Heaven is just this:

twined strands
of winking bulbs

and shiny, fragile ornaments
understood to represent grace

weakly.

It's all this:

the paleness of representation,
the understanding,

the fond sadness it causes,

the shining
circularity.

2

That morning he fell asleep on the couch, or seemed to, giggling
himself awake repeatedly, once saying, "Orange hair! Orange hair
is orangutan hair!"

*

Or when we were in bed, he throwing me into a new position
every few seconds as if frantically searching for something.

*

I followed him to the store because he'd been gone too long. As I rounded the corner, he was just coming out, but, instead of turning toward home, he went into the parking lot, scanning it. I noticed his walk was different.

*

He always said my poems were lonely, as if each thing (word, person) stood still, waiting for meaning.

3

I think your homeland
is in sleep's vicinity.

There's some reiterative
noodling
in absentia,

almost "brush-clad."

Can you tell me
what I'm seeing?

There's a sound like voices there
singing, "Don't worry."

Does that make any sense
to you?

I think you're being escorted
between "woe"
and "woven."

Then the tip encysts
where a search
has been called off

THE FIT

In a fit of repugnance
each moment
rips itself in half,

producing a twin.

*

In a coming-of-age story
each dream
produces me:

an ignorance
on the point of revelation.

*

I'm at a side table

in a saloon
in Alaska,

my eye on the door
where a flood of strangers
pours in.

*

The door or the window?

It's morning.

The story is told from the view-point of two young technicians, one fat and one thin, who must give their superior a moment by moment account of their attempts to monitor the subject. Suspense occurs, occasionally, when they must tell the superior that they're having trouble keeping the listening devices within range. We sympathize with the hunted subject, but also with the clearly competent, frequently exasperated technicians, whose situation is, after all, much more like our own.

SOLID

I

To produce the consistency of experience,

each night
the program toys with the idea
that the picture might be doctored:

it's the false monster in the lake
known as George Washington.

What "lake?"

*

I submerge

because I enjoy
waking up,

arising
from chaos

bit by bit
again.

The "ness"
that is nothing*ness*,

but seen from within.

"Nude activists in Berkeley
find the law
has them covered."

"Hero surfaces
from sunken sub,"
                              it says.

When we come back,
"Southern Exposure:

radiation leak

The Night
The Lights Went Out In Georgia."

                    *

When we come back,
the murdered siblings

reappear
as trolls and elves.

When we come back,
the heir apparent

crafts
his solid victory

CO-EXISTENCE

Transparency's the joke
a text tells an audience
with which it may
or may not
co-exist.

     *

"Existence" is weak,
start again.

     *

Hey,

watch me say
"Hi Fishy!"

someone shouts.

But I'm crossing my "K"s

     *

The individual
with flukes

in her brain
will climb

to the top of a grass blade
and wait

until eaten
by a grazing cow

ENTANGLEMENT

I

"Don't let the car fool you.

My treasure
is in heaven."

2

The material world is made up
entirely

of collisions

between otherwise
indefinite objects.

Then what *is* a collision?

(Or the physical world
collapses

into place

at the shock of
being seen.)

3

In the shorter version,

tentacled
stomach swallows stomach.

In a long dream,
I'm with Aaron,

visiting his future,
helping him make choices.

MY ADVANTAGE

Can a dreamer
outwit her dream?

Not on a first date.

*

One dream is a fake small town.

Its diner is through the attic door in the home of a couple I know.
They show me the stairs while continuing a low-grade quarrel. This
diner is where tonight's game will be played.

I've come to deliver a score keeping belt but, not knowing how
it works, I can't help feeling strange.

*

In an adjacent dream,
a woman from work

hands me a slew of wrapped presents.
Two contain napkins, but

then there's a newborn
cat in the third. She's testing me.

"I don't need to see the rest," I say.
" I can assume redundancy."

When she smiles
in acknowledgment,
I press my advantage—

insisting she take it all
back to her estate.

END TIMES

1

Galaxies run from us. "Don't look!"
Was this the meaning
of the warning in the Garden?
When a dreamer sees she's dreaming,
it causes figments to disperse.

2

Black bars and dots
of low cloud,

almost a signature,
reflected on a sunset marsh.

Luxuriant and spurious code

as art,
as if we were meant to think,

"Beautiful!"—
so we do

and a ripple
travels in one spot.

When something reaches
the speed of light

it will appear to freeze,

growing gradually
less meaningful.

Being able to look at water soothes the anxious emptiness be-
tween thoughts. I think again and again about the way the water
looks. I can keep each thought longer by writing it down. The
process of writing this sentence is time-consuming in itself, al-
most irritatingly slow—so now I rush and jumble the letters. It
occurs to me that later I may not be able to read what I wrote.

SECONDS

1

The point is to see through
the dying,

who pinch non-existent
objects from the air

sequentially,

to this season's
laying on of
withered leaves?

2

A moment is everything

one person

(see below)

takes in simultaneously

though some

or much of what

a creature feels

may not reach

conscious awareness

and only a small part

(or none) of this

will be carried forward

to the next instant.

3

Any one
not seconded

burns up in rage.

THE CELL PHONE AT YOUR EAR MAY NOT EXIST

"You know what, take this down.

How you doing, lady, you doing okay?

Cause I got your name in my phone book.

I was talking to someone before

and her name was something like that.

I'm just here, kicking back.

Coffee shop, barber shop. Yeah,

it's gonna be alright

cause your name's right here. Okay?"

    *

Is quotation vicious?
Poignant?

A chicken head
is winking,

sipping through a straw
from the "u"

in "regular"

One's a connoisseur of vacancies,

loud silences
surrounding human artifacts:

 stucco hulls
of forgotten origin

that squat
over the sleepers

in rows
on raised platforms.

She calls her finds
"encapsulations."

            *

One is ebullient,

shaving seconds,
navigating among refills.

She's concerned with the rhythm
of her own sequence of events,

if such they can be called,

though these may be indistinguishable
from those in the lives of other people,

though the continuity which interests her
breaks up
in the middle distance.

*

She finds the fly-leaves of her new notebook
have been pre-printed
in old-fashioned script—

phrases broken to suggest
mid-race

as a site of faux urgency:

"this work since it's commenced"

"cannot nor willnot stay"

IN TIME

1

To start things off

our parent
might have used music

to make drama
out of symmetry,

as if each side
of the body

asked the other one,
"How long?"

2

If only

extenuation
could be teased

into pulse-like
flutters. Frills.

"To frill"
meaning forget oneself,

"oneself" meaning one's place
in line.

Here an ad
for Merit cigarettes

shows a rhino
on a frozen pond.

What can time do
but pass?

Here "to pass"
is the same as
"to exist" :

a ghostly appendage
of uncertain length.

INTERIOR DESIGN

1

Whistles
tussle in the canopy.

Beginners
are being taught to think,

drawing straight lines
between dots
to reveal hidden shapes

and punish
rounded extras briskly.

Sculpted cumulus,
whipped cream.

(A thought
is a wish for relation
doubling as a boundary.)

2

Fetish objects
now occur
as previous centuries.

Miniature log cabins
beside the jelly cabinet.

These are just what we've needed
to fortify our love.

NEXT GENERATIONS

I

But, on "Star Trek," we *aren't* the Borg,

the aggressive conglomerate,

each member part humanoid, part

machine, bent on assimilating

foreign cultures. In fact,

we destroy their ship,

night after night,

in preparation for sleep.

2

We sense something's wrong

when our ideal selves

look like contract players.

The captain plays what's left

of believable authority

as a Shakespearean actor.

The rest are there to show surprise

each time

the invading cube appears—

until any response seems stupid.

But we forgive them.

We've made camp

in the glitch

INTACT

    I

From what I don't recall
I am able to infer
what didn't happen
in a given setting

while you can't or won't

so that
I might have been behind you
in the boat
or you might have been alone
or accompanied by strangers.

Alternates persist
since they aren't named as such.

On the other hand, I feel
the removal of one element
changes the event
so it must disappear

      (intact)

    2

If thunder clapped,

small flowers
at leaf joints

stared straight ahead
in silence.

Did rocks react?

Try to recall

If sadness
is akin to patience,

we're back!

Pattern recognition
was our first response

to loneliness.

Here and there were *like*
one place.

But we need to triangulate,
find someone to show.

   *

There's a jolt, quasi-electric,
when one of our myths
reverts to abstraction.

Now we all know
every name's Eurydice,
briefly returned
from blankness

and the way back
won't bear scrutiny.

High voices
over rapid-pulsing synthesizers
intone, "without you"—

which is soothing.

We prefer meta-significance:

the way the clouds exchange
white scraps
in glory.

No more wishes.

No more bungalows
behind car-washes
painted the color of
swimming pools

MANY

Gull
or jet—

some attention momentarily
recreated
in its own image

rides
the extended,
stiffened past.

                *

This morning twin webs
map fresh horizontals
over blunt bamboo stalks—

you're only as good as
the more recent.

                *

A large man twists his torso,
raises both forearms alongside,
and yawns.

Sun slicks the square tops
of black window bars.

"Who are you talking to?"

I'm finding my balance.

38

*

Letters throw lassos
far below
at pen tip:

bacteria's
tell-tale thought-bubbles
in the sediment.

*

It's the way the eight legs
can neither line up nor
come abreast,

each entering the present
in its own good time,

that spooks us.

ONCE

I

Once there were people among whom
each one had to be convinced
she was the most wondrous alive
in order to go on living.
It was creation ex nihilo
all over again.
Crews were organized in shifts.
"Skin as white as snow
and hair as black as night," they chanted.
In off hours, everyone smirked
at the result
and called it sentimental.

2

At last the camp melodrama
of Dan Rather

relaxes

into the pseudo
sibling raillery
of the local newscast.

Since we're being escorted
from moment to moment

by what's already
familial,

we should be able
to follow this track
back

home
to our previous thought.

3

The opposite
of nothingness

is direction

"You can tell 'em
               I'll
        be
there"

in the old songs
where verbs stand around,
edgy,
between hungry ghosts.

     *

Woman in a sing-song voice:

"I *coulda* gone
to the fabric store
alone . . ."

but what but what but what but what

     *

Relive the dream
with Grace Slick.

     *

Light stays light

but "toward"
becomes unclear.

*

(Bush stumps
for agenda

amid giant redwoods.)

*

I don't mind
learning
I'm in hell

if
I can learn it
again and again

TRANSACTION

Tracts amenable
to brief description.

Light finds the quickest route

and the mind tries
to see patterns.

What do these things have in common?

They behave as if
impatient.

    *

As he takes your order,
the fast-food clerk says,
"I can hook you up."

Fish shaped like pencils
or tattered stars
patrol the small aquarium.

(The whole being
of the sophisticated person
is an answer to questions
not immediately posed.)

Marvin Gaye's "What's Going On"
is batted back
and forth
between speakers.

*

One says, "Without question."

Or "I enjoyed every minute of it."

Or "Dachau rocked my world." And

as for me,

I'm pure hatred.

*

The impulse
on which ice-plant fingers
fork

and hibiscus opens
its dry mouths
to yawn—

screw "unison"—

get it and go on

FLINCH

A new season
sweeps across the merchandise.

Paper products suggest harvest,
then fear of the dark.

Rows of palms
in stanchions
abstain,

having little stake
in matter.

They flap their fronds weakly
as we revolve.

*

Is it true we deserve
any blow
we fail to anticipate?

A shadow
traveling down a wall

is a maternal hand

while a maternal hand
is lavender-suffusing
dusk

and dusk itself,
a great tissue
of lies,

suffused with blood.

*

Three things are placed
in safety

on a created plane:

twilight
and the stop-gap palms
bellwether palms

advance

with the transparent
cloud-scarves
of the nonexistent

fatalistic nomads
we half-dreamed
            of being

WRITE HOME

In order to write
you must fall in love

with your own thought
every time.

    *

The dream was a sealed
capsule

in bed, sending out
reports reading:

"Wonce" "We" "Warn" "Won."
Waking

ready to record
but sad

as if each repeated
letter

were merely
the bearer of nostalgia

"Boy Wins Love With Tall Tale."

The fundamental
stuff of matter

is the Liar's
Paradox.

Mass is a function
of frequency

and frequency
is a matter

of counting up to what?

*

The celebrity spokesman
for 911

gives his name
to an emergency

operator who refuses
to believe

he's who he says he is.
An ironic

detachment

forms the centerpiece
of his new act.

We double back
to form thoughts.

"Umbilical Stump Still Pulses."

Now the toothless man
in fringed leather
looks over his shoulder
at them kindly.

Now the very
fabric
of space

is an agreement
to agree.

"We're looking for the coincidence
detector
that lets cells know
they've fired simultaneously."

*

One believes she moves
forward

by absorbing
what has just occurred.

One thinks
he's the space
he clears.

*

They tell this story
about themselves:

Fashion
is the big business

of making way
for what comes next

though this next thing's
not important,

not terribly important
yet

AS ONE

1

After months apart, my friend invites me to meet her at a tourist spot in the town where we both used to live. We sit at a table in the sun, behind a mariachi band, and speak rapidly, as if trying to "catch up." She says that what scientists are learning about time suggests it may be possible to see into the future. I agree by mangling quotes from Gödel and Hawking. "If the entire universe is spinning—and why not?—time may be circular." We interrupt each other frequently, as if excited, though, in fact, we have had this conversation several times before.

2

Harsh words come to mind,
"burst in uninvited."
They may refer to me,

but I speak them aloud
to myself, by myself,

which makes them less convincing

3

"There are really only two
ideas."

A) We can be represented,
someone can take our place or suffer
in our stead.

B) This has happened already, in the distant past,
and all we need do is recall it.

Having a thought
    that a sound
        is a truck.

Having a thought:
    it's the chorus
        of a Beach Boys' song-

Round round
    Get around
        I get around

Head swiveling
    Alarm. Then mock-alarm
        For one life-time

THIS TIME

1

It seemed normal.

Just last minute's
hard scrabble of brush
                    left out—

and now laced
with rollicking flickers.

What?

With unwound cassette tape.

Or tape wound
stick to stick
to send the last signal.

2

Dreams write themselves.

The sense of being addressed
lasts minutes.

The milkweed weaves itself
an empty cotton dress. Then

a tiny woman
comes out at the top.

She brings the people
their first map

in the form of a spider's web.

This time
no one is suspicious.

INTERVAL

We flex
to create coordinates.

How often in dreams
I'm making my point
clear—

some point
I've never wanted to make
before or since—

and to acquaintances
vividly called up
for the occasion.

"Picture time
as a fine mesh

of regular intervals."
But are those intervals

like bits of thread,
their intersections

or the empty squares between?
"Interval" suggests music.

I'm getting ready
for the possibility

that a rhythm
will be monotonous,

relentless.

EN ROUTE

We've re-authorized silence
as a bridge
between two notes—

so that we're always
"about to" or
"have just."

    *

So that a magic school bus
bounces
through a haunted museum.

    *

A small boy
stops his ears with both hands

then spreads his arms wide,

covers his eyes
then flings his hands apart

like a performer concluding a set.

"What does a cat say?"
his mother asks.

Reading, we are allowed to follow someone else's train of thought as it starts off for an imaginary place. This train has been produced for us—or rather materialized and extended until it is almost nothing like the ephemeral realizations with which we're familiar. To see words pulled one by one into existence is to intrude on a privacy of sorts. But we *are* familiar with the contract between spectator and performer. Now the text isn't a train but an actress/model who takes off her school uniform piece by piece alone with the cameraman. She's a good girl playing at being bad, all the time knowing better. She invites us to join her in that knowledge. But this is getting us nowhere.

No problem

and an infinite number
of solutions:

woman dressed as "Frank N Furter"
from The Rocky Horror Picture Show

alone on the sidewalk, 9:30 a.m.,
August 24, 2002.

　　　　*

Pillar of smoke.

Pillar of small stones
at the conclusion

of a street divider,
one upended on top—

the desire to talk

trapped there
in a small case letter "i"

or an inverted exclamation mark.

　　　　*

Pleased as if
what can be condensed

could be returned
by the same gesture
to its point of origin

where *I* could cause it
to break out again

from a single word.

*

"Events remembered
include famous fires."

1

Sure, the captain's caught
in an "energy field,"
but who hasn't
been turned to stone
by watching
the outlandish get-ups
of our recent past
re-run?

2

"I am that
I am"

broken

into bits,
each one accusing,

"You've completely lost it!"

3

Next to us, an ancient couple
uses baby-talk
to mock each other's intonations

and, through the window,
stiff, rough, pink-trimmed,
matched, green tongues of flame.

BOX

Pulling up to the minute,

think, "Mental detritus."

Picking up speed,

the craze for useless crazes

is a joke about something—

but what?

Bird rides wire—

a probe

in the cold stir.

Falling asleep, I hear that

"only one hill works."

We laugh

to accommodate death.

Dream someone's placed me

in a red, plastic box

from which now I pop up,

clown-like,

into consciousness.

A time when we agree

the present does not exist,

has never existed.

Black puffs drift

in front of salmon smears—

sky going white beyond.

I'll be called up

from moment to moment

to decide

what's plausible.

It is terrible

to die—

but for a thought

not to be thought?

1

Almost all the words we've said to one another are gone
and if they were retrieved, verbatim, we might not acknowledge
them.
But the *tenor* of our talk
has been constant across decades!
(Tenor is what we meant by "soul.")

For instance,
the way we joke
by using non-sequiturs, elliptical remarks
which deliberately suppress context
in advance
of time's rub-out.

2

"When size really counts,"
the billboard says

showing the product
tiny,

in one corner,

so we need to search for it.
Come find me.

I stand
behind these words.

PHRASING

    I

"Let's really show the world
that we're getting warmed up."

A certain ambient
despair
washes the stomach gently.

"Let us disguise
eternity

as a survival
drama.

How will consciousness
be organized

when material grows scarce

after the death
of stars?"

Into flaps? Pulsations?

Shell-game urgency
of the news-hour.

What pumps to the surface
is all empty

circle-skirt,

a scalloped
white-pink thing.

The trick is to turn it
inside out?

2

What *are* words for?
To be put in order,

time disentangled from space.

So when I get there,
there's no one around –

just a phrase
somewhere,

hearing itself
think,

whistling up and down
its forecast
of a scale

while twigs make
minor adjustments.

"I'm in between
two states
and can't be interrupted,

between two points
and can't be found,

waylaid

Thus the palm is rakish

and the philodendron
lugubrious.

Only using such rare words
will justify

my writing *this*,

my writing "my"
or *now*

here

BACK

68

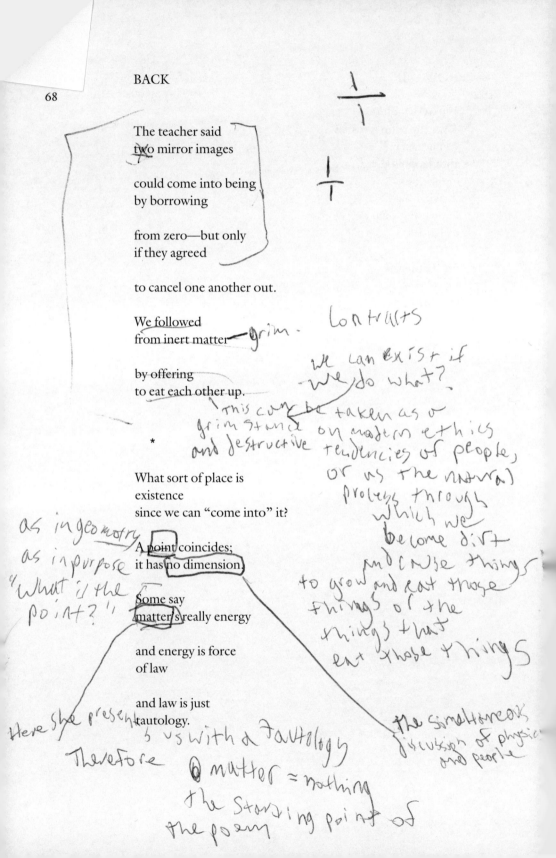

The teacher said
two mirror images

could come into being
by borrowing

from zero—but only
if they agreed

to cancel one another out.

We followed
from inert matter — grim.

by offering
to eat each other up.

*

What sort of place is
existence
since we can "come into" it?

A point coincides;
it has no dimension.

Some say
matter's really energy

and energy is force
of law

and law is just
tautology.

Therefore

Handwritten annotations:

Contrasts

we can exist if
we do what?

This can be taken as a
grim stance on modern ethics
and destructive tendencies of people,
or as the natural
process through
which we
become dirt
and cause things
to grow and eat those
things or the
things that
eat those things

as in geometry
as in purpose
"what is the
point?"

Here she presents
us with a tautology

Therefore matter = nothing
the starting point of
the poem

the simultaneous
discussion of physics
and people

*

We were taught

to have faces
by a face

looking "back"

The Mirror stage

Jacques Lacan

— reflection

Abortionist